VERY ANNOYING PEOPLE

...on your train

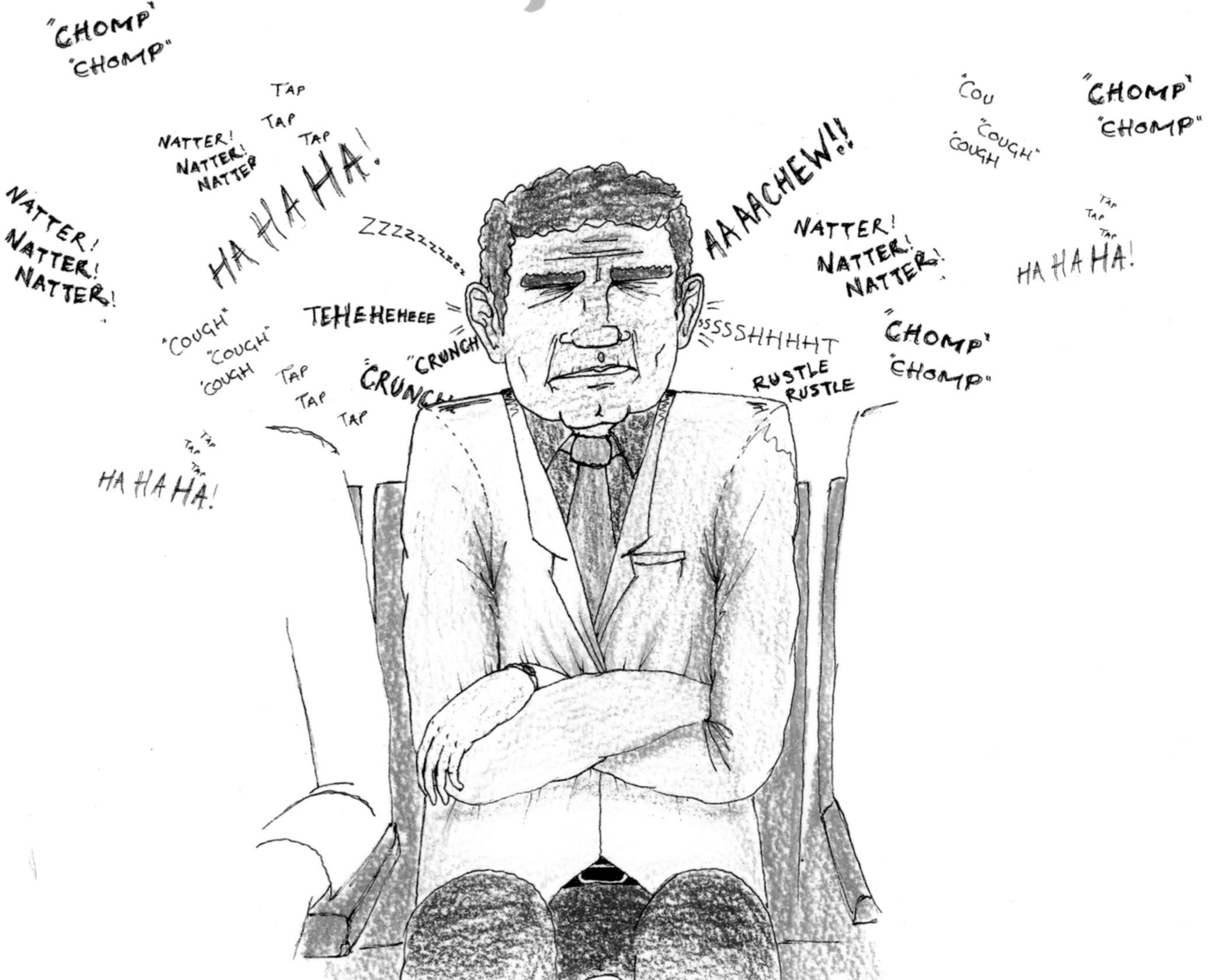

Published by Phil Elson
First CreateSpace Edition 2018

Interior and cover design: Cassia Friello
Illustrations: Greg Wallaker

Dedicated to my wonderful son, William.

When you grow up and start going to work, I hope you find something to do for a living that you really love - and I *really* hope that, whatever it is, it doesn't involve wasting your life sitting on commuter trains for three hours a day!

Phil Elson lives with his wife and son in a beautiful part of Surrey in England. He has a Bachelors Degree with Honours in Sociology from Salford University in Greater Manchester and a 4.0-grade Masters Degree in Management from Stevens Institute of Technology in Hoboken, NJ. He grew up in England, but worked in New York for 14 years, before moving to St. Petersburg, Russia for a year. In 2009 he moved back to England.

Phil has built up a successful career working in aviation insurance since 1988. He holds US and UK citizenship, has visited over 100 countries and has a tested IQ of 155 (which he doesn't like to show off about).

Why is it that as soon as some people enter a railway station they seem to forget their basic manners and behave so poorly?

Anyone who regularly uses a train, *and definitely everyone on my commuter trains to and from London each day*, will have come across this phenomenon and recognise many of the selfish little behaviours listed in this book.

So as you read through the descriptions and look at the pictures, you'll probably discover you are already very well acquainted with many of the characters. Maybe one of them is sitting opposite you in the train carriage right now as you read? Take some comfort in the fact that you are not alone in getting upset with them! Consider turning to the page that shows their particular transgression. Then perhaps passive-aggressively dangle it in front of them so they can see it.

Or perhaps you know someone who frequently travels by rail and complains bitterly about it? If that's the case, please show them this book out of compassion. The realisation that they are not alone, and they in fact share in a very common problem with millions of others, will no doubt be deeply cathartic and will go a long way to healing their emotional wounds.

Finally, here's something for you to consider: If you regularly take a train - and are entirely honest with yourself - might you even recognise one or two of these bad behaviours *within you*? If so, don't feel down about it, because this book is here to provide you with a golden opportunity to acknowledge your faults and then make some simple changes in your life that will help you achieve real personal growth.

If you stop acting out even just one of these antisocial behaviours on the train, I assure you that you will significantly reduce the overall negative energy in the world, whilst instantly becoming a slightly better human being - and one who your fellow passengers will hold in the highest regard (albeit probably in the form of silent admiration).

And wouldn't that be a great result for everyone?

Phil Elson

The Annoy-o-meter

What bad behaviour on the trains bothers you the most? As you read through the categories in this book, get in touch with your inner-most feelings and give each one a rating on your own personal "Annoy-o-meter":

Simply take a pen or pencil and draw on the dial where you think it should be like this:

Then compare your answers amongst your friends!

1. Dithering Danny

Evidently, he has no idea how to successfully operate a ticket machine or navigate his way through a barrier.

Even though he's in his 40's, this appears to be the first time he's ever taken a train ride in his life.

And now you're stood right behind him, watching him floundering, as your train slowly pulls away on the other side.

ANNOY-O-METER

2. Coffee Breath Seth

Every morning, Seth orders his favourite drink to start his day. But he's blissfully unaware of the havoc that his flat white extra shot soyachino is wreaking on his fellow passengers.

Stinking of a lethal mixture of coffee and pooh, please don't be afraid to offer him a mint!

ANNOY-O-METER

3. Sneezy Pete

With such a heavy streaming cold, he really should have stayed at home - not for *his* sake but for *ours*.

Pete makes half-hearted attempts to cover up his massive sneezes by waving his hand about 12 inches in-front of his nose - but that only serves to spread the millions of tiny sneeze particles over an even wider area.

ANNOY-O-METER

4. The Bowling Pins

Every morning your train lumbers into the station, already packed to the rafters. 100 regular commuters at your stop have long ago worked out exactly where each door will open.

So every few metres groups of around ten people stand huddled together in little triangles, like bowling pins, all facing the front and eagerly waiting for the doors to open so they can surge in. Newcomers don't have a chance getting on - unless perhaps they've brought along a 7 kg bowling ball to throw at the nearest group!

ANNOY-O-METER

5. Tardy Tanya

She's really late getting off at her stop – so a huge group of passengers has to wait for her, until the doors are just about to close, before they can finally get onboard.

But Tanya's doing just fine!

ANNOY-O-METER

6. Doorway Danny

Has no idea he's holding up the entire train by straddling the open doorway, as the doors continually half close and reopen again and again behind him...

ANNOY-O-METER

7. Timothy Tiny-Bike

Even though it's not a full-sized bicycle it still takes up loads of space, so three people can't get on.

For goodness sake, just get a proper bike and cycle all the way to work!

ANNOY-O-METER

8. Snoring Simon

He's had such an early start, getting on the 6:45. Time to catch up on some zzzzz's – at everyone else's expense.

ANNOY-O-METER

11

9. Open Yawn Dawn

"Why would I possibly put my hand over my mouth when I'm doing a big public yawn in the morning?"

"Look and marvel at my dentistry!"

ANNOY-O-METER

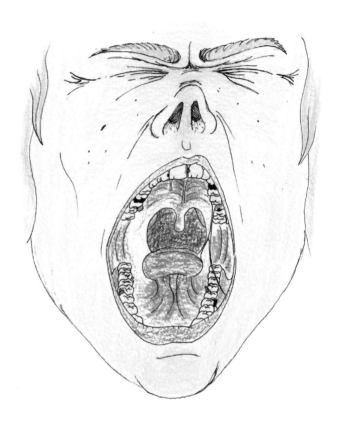

10. Sally Seat Keeper

Yes, it's entirely possible to loathe and resent a bag...

"I'm sorry, this seat is taken. My friend just texted me to say he'll be joining the train in six stops' time."

ANNOY-O-METER

11. Broadsheet Bill

He's reading an old-style newspaper with his arms spread open as wide as can be - without a care in the world.

Get with the modern age, Grandad, and get on the Internet with a phone.

ANNOY-O-METER

12. "Lippy" Lisa

Half asleep in the morning. Inexpertly using her eyelash curler and then crudely applying smears of make-up with the use of a tiny mirror, as the train bumps along to the city.

Lisa boards the train in her home town as a "4", but gets off in the terminus as a solid "7".

ANNOY-O-METER

13. Bumpin' Bass Brian

Playing his incredibly loud bass music through highly inefficient noise-leaking headphones. Now we can all enjoy the sick beatz!

ANNOY-O-METER

14. Stoic Cynthia

80 years old and standing right next to where you're sitting.

You repeatedly offer Cynthia your seat, but she politely declines each time.

Unfortunately, no-one else hears this brief verbal exchange, so they all think you're an inconsiderate monster.

ANNOY-O-METER

14

15. Larry the Laptop

Sitting in a four-seat section, Larry is working on a spreadsheet - and taking over the entire table with his computer and various open files.

Surely that's a breach of his company's IT policy? And wouldn't it just be terrible if the train jerked and you spilt your coffee all over his machine?

ANNOY-O-METER

16. Comfortable Chloe

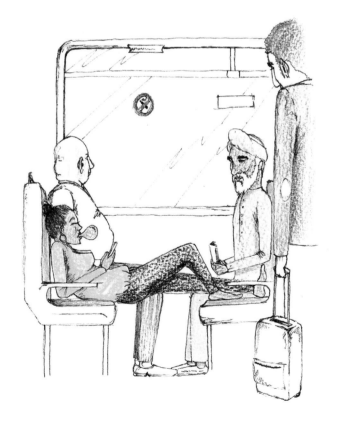

This cheerless teenager can always be found sitting with her feet up on the seat in-front. Nothing's going to move Chloe – she's very comfortable!

ANNOY-O-METER

17. Mr. Licky Fingers

Got 90 minutes to kill, sitting in a hot, sweaty, packed train carriage?... Time to break out the family pack of cheese and onion crisps! Rustle, crackle, crunch, crunch - as he stinks up the carriage.

"Don't forget to lick all the revolting crisp dust off your fingers, sir!"

ANNOY-O-METER

18. Pervy Patricia

At first glance she looks perfectly decent and respectable. But then you catch a glimpse of the total mummy-porn filth she's reading in her women's magazine!

"How to drive your partner wild" doesn't sound like a proper news article to me...

ANNOY-O-METER

19. Hacking Henry

The guy you just sat opposite seemed perfectly normal for the first ten seconds... but now he starts hacking out violent death-coughs every 30 seconds in your general direction.

Henry barely makes an attempt to cover up his mouth, and frankly, he's doing a far from stellar job of shielding everyone from his germs.

ANNOY-O-METER

20. Stealthy Sophie

She's more than happy to sneak out the odd silent little chuff when the mood takes her – but people often blame the guy sitting next to her.

At least they're silent – nobody wants to hear a sound like a wardrobe being intermittently dragged across a hardwood floor!

ANNOY-O-METER

21. First Class Franky

I know I shouldn't judge people, but this rough-looking teenager doesn't exactly look like he should be sitting in the first class section!

ANNOY-O-METER

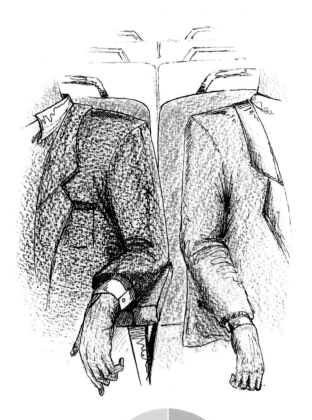

ANNOY-O-METER

22. Eddy the Elbow

Extremely territorial. He insists on putting his elbow on the armrest, even though you were using it before he even got on.

Then with every micro-movement of the train, he inches his way slowly into total control of the rest. Eddy secretly fights this war every day! His arm is now locked in place and *will not* be budged. You just know that's all he's thinking about throughout the entire journey.

23. Fugly Karen / Flugly Ken

Oh dear - You've got to stare across at *that* for the next hour.

ANNOY-O-METER

24. Creepy Craig

Commuting just got a lot more interesting for Craig, since he bought himself his new mini camera.

Craig needs to be arrested!

ANNOY-O-METER

25. Fainting Frances

If you cast your minds back far enough, years ago, we would have had a lot of sympathy for Frances when she passed out in a hot steamy carriage on a summer's day.

Certainly not these days! Quite simply, Frances is now what's stopping you from getting to work on time.

ANNOY-O-METER

26. "Chuckles" the Driver's Assistant

Hanging onto one last shred of humanity by attempting to crack a joke over the loudspeaker, as he announces the *delay du jour*.

Commuters listen and smile awkwardly to each other, not wanting to look like they're too mean-spirited to join in this lowest form of "fun.

ANNOY-O-METER

27. Busy Bill

He's a top salesman with a very important business call to make – which must be carried out at *full* volume for everyone to hear.

"Yeah............. Yeah....... Don't worry, it's on our radar and we've got the bandwidth to cope with that........... Look, we're all singing from the same hymn sheet here, Derek............ Fantastic - I'll ping you an email by close of play and we'll touch base again tomorrow!"

ANNOY-O-METER

28. Irate Rita

It's the end of the work day. The trains are all cancelled and she's angry as hell.

Sighing. Constantly checking the timetable on her smartphone app and calling home to give her partner a running commentary on the unfolding chaos.

"Signal failure again? That's it! We're moving to the countryside and opening up a llama sanctuary!"

ANNOY-O-METER

29. Smart-phone Simon

How is he able to do a two-hour commute either way without once looking up from his smartphone screen, which is permanently situated six inches from his face?

This miraculous feat includes a half-mile walk from the office, a long train ride to his home town and even a drive home from the station car park! And how come he never once loses his signal or gets a flat battery?

ANNOY-O-METER

30. B.O. Joe

It's been a long, hot day in the city. Joe is relaxing on the train. He isn't working any more today – but unfortunately, the same is true for his deoderant!

ANNOY-O-METER

31. Spacey Stacey

She's standing halfway down the carriage aisle - with dozens of people packed in on one side of her – *but metres of empty space on the other side.*

Stacey is somehow oblivious to the fact that, because she won't move down the carriage to the end, 30 people have to be wedged into the door area.

But Stacey has a nemesis...

ANNOY-O-METER

32. Window Tappin' Tony

Standing on the platform, furiously rat-tat-tatting on the window, shouting out to Spacey Stacey "Move down the carriage, for goodness sake – we're all trying to get home!"

Impotent rage at its finest!

ANNOY-O-METER

33. Lars & Lindy

They've just arrived from abroad for two weeks' vacation.

On the train up from the airport, there they sit, occupying eight seats with their array of suitcases - seemingly oblivious to the fact that hundreds of daily commuters are standing next to them, squashed in the aisle.

ANNOY-O-METER

34. Daisy's Dog

Even though it's an animal, it gets to sit on one of the seats for *humans*.

That's because Daisy knows that *her* dog is special, while all the poor, exhausted, ticket-paying people standing around are *not*.

ANNOY-O-METER

35. Backpack Bernie

What *is* he carrying in that huge bag?

Why doesn't he take that massive thing off his shoulder, so it's not constantly bumping into me?

These days, there's an awful lot of Backpack Bernies and Bernardettes.

ANNOY-O-METER

36. The Train Hiker

He got on last, just before the train left. But starting in Carriage 12, he then feels the need to make his way immediately to Carriage 1 through packed aisles while the train is moving.

"Excuse me! Coming through. Excuse me please!..."

ANNOY-O-METER

37. Unstable Mabel

To her, standing still in a gently rocking train is like attempting to stand upright on a rowing boat in a hurricane. Oops! We're braking again. Careful she doesn't land on you!

Mabel probably needs to get her inner ears checked.

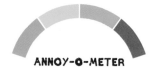

ANNOY-O-METER

38. Armpit Arnold

Standing over a foot taller than you, he's grabbing the handrail directly over your head, his damp armpit constantly nudging directly into your face, in a rhythmic motion, as the train sways back and forth.

Ahhh – lovely!

ANNOY-O-METER

39. Nosy Nigel

Years ago this wouldn't have been quite so bad, because people would just read other people's newspaper or book on the train. But now our technology has made it so much more personal...

"What's this woman next to me doing?... Sending private texts to her mum who's not well? Hmmm, interesting! Think I'll just lean in a bit and read over her shoulder.

ANNOY-O-METER

40. Les Enfants Terribles

A group of 30 excitable teenage foreign exchange students descend onto one carriage, all shouting at each other. To their credit, they all seem happy, energetic and amazingly self-confident.

At least *they* seem to be having a good time!

ANNOY-O-METER

41. Zone-Out Zachery

Sunglasses, raised scarf, cap and over-sized headphones – and that blank stare into the middle distance. Zach certainly has his own way of coping with the stress and tedium of commuting to and from the city.

But with that amount of sensory deprivation, he'll probably miss his stop!

ANNOY-O-METER

42. "Shoulders"

Huge oversized bodybuilder type with arms held in a wide arc, as if carrying invisible logs under them – not a problem in itself. But all the steroids have made him hyper-aggressive when anyone accidently brushes past him.

ANNOY-O-METER

43. Flashy Fergus

Fergus is very proud of his high-end designer watch.

He often actually *prefers* to stand and hold the overhead handrail, as this allows him to surreptitiously lift his sleeve to reveal his pride and joy to all.

ANNOY-O-METER

RS   MIN

44. Widespread Wayne

Unlike the rest of us, he finds it physically impossible to sit with his legs closed in a normal fashion. They must always be pointing in a wide "v" - much to the dismay of the person sharing his double seat.

ANNOY-O-METER

45. Mr. Pick & Eat (a.k.a. "The Bogey Man")

Getting hungry halfway through the journey? This guy knows where to go for a delicious snack - up his own nose!

The alternative is even worse - when not peckish, he will often wipe his nose detritus on the seat-back table in-front of him for future passengers to enjoy.

ANNOY-O-METER

46. Hungry Harry

A few beers after work and Harry needs to eat his dinner on the train journey home.

Unfortunately for everyone else in the carriage, the main station's culinary options are severely limited. So Harry tucks into a particularly pungent Chicken Curry Cornish Pasty. Thank you Harry!

ANNOY-O-METER

47. Pebble-dash Pete

He couldn't help himself when they offered him a big plate of oysters at the business lunch - and now he's on his way home - looking forlornly down the crowded corridor at the occupied toilet at the far end.

Nobody goes for a "Number Two" on the train unless there's something seriously wrong. Pete knows in his heart that he's probably not going to make it in time.

ANNOY-O-METER

48. The Football Friends

These cheeky, happy-go-lucky, fun-loving lads are just off for a bit of a laugh at today's big game on the other side of the city. "F*** this" and "F*** that" - they know they're being a little bit rowdy!

What they don't know is that everyone else thinks they're just f***ing annoying.

ANNOY-O-METER

49. Scary Teenagers

"I don't normally get on the 'local' train through all the inner city stops, so tonight's long journey home, stopping every other minute, is a rare treat!"

But why are these local gangsta 'kidz' all talking in Jamaican patois when they're white?

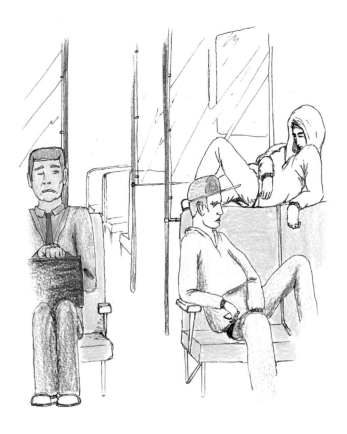

ANNOY-O-METER

50. Paul the Partyman

He's usually a little worse for wear after a long night out with his colleagues, standing in a bar and drinking for six hours straight. Paul sees no reason to end the fun when he gets on the train, so he loads up with cans of lager.

Maybe it's time for a nap? – unfortunately, that could mean his head slumped on your shoulder until you reach you stop!

ANNOY-O-METER

51. The Chatty Friends

What a coincidence! They've just bumped into each other after such a long time. Now they have so much to catch up on, as they witter away endlessly.

You are sat next to them, trying to: (a) read your book, (b) catch up on some work emails, or (c) simply concentrate on just how much you hate your commute and life.

(Ok, this one is pretty mean-spirited)

ANNOY-O-METER

52. Tutting Toby

Toby sits there in silent judgement of everyone else in the carriage. There's probably quite a few "Tobys" on most trains.

Are *you* sometimes one of them?

ANNOY-O-METER

I would very much like to thank Greg Wallaker for his truly amazing drawings, Cassia Friello for her beautiful book design and Roland Moore and Josh Mendham for helping me with the edit. Of course, I also need to thank all the millions of frustrated, weary and downtrodden rail passengers around the world, with whom I have a common bond through our shared understanding of the misery of daily commuting by train. And finally, I must give a big thank you to all the thousands of people on trains who regularly display such self-centred and selfish behaviour with complete disregard for the people around them. Without you this book would not have been possible.

Printed by Amazon Italia Logistica S.r.l.
Torrazza Piemonte (TO), Italy

13524354R00020